COMPACT DISC PAGE AND BAND INFORMATION

MMO CD 3615

mmo Music Minus One

ORCHESTRAL GEMS FOR CLASSICAL GUITAR

Band No. Complete Version		Band No. Minus Guitar	Page No.
1	*Tschaikovsky:* Chanson Triste	11	4
2	*Korsakov:* Song Of India	12	7
3	*Iradier:* La Paloma	13	10
4	*Lehar:* Vilia	14	12
5	*Bizet:* Adagietto (L'Arlesienne Suite)	15	14
6	*Foster:* Old Folks At Home	16	16
7	*Traditional:* Drink To Me Only With Thine Eyes	17	18
8	*Gruber:* Silent Night	18	19
9	*Offenbach:* Barcarolle	19	20
10	- Tuning Notes: A440		

Chanson Triste

PYOTR IL'YICH TSCHAIKOVSKY

Guitar

Andantino

tap tap tap tap

*The tablature staff displays the most accessible fingering for the beginning student, which may vary from those chosen by the soloist.

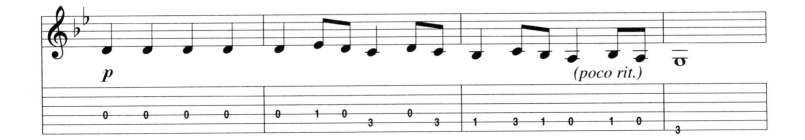

ORCHESTRAL GEMS
For
CLASSICAL GUITAR

Chanson Triste	Tschaikovsky
Song Of India	Rimsky-Korsakov
La Paloma	Sebastian Iradier
Vilia	Franz Lehar
Adagietto	Georges Bizet
Old Folks At Home	Stephen Foster
Drink To Me Only With Thine Eyes	Traditional
Silent Night	Franz Gruber
Barcarolle	Jules Offenbach

3615

PRINTED IN CANADA

A tempo

*If 3 note chord voicing is too difficult, the highest pitch (F) can be substituted.

A tempo

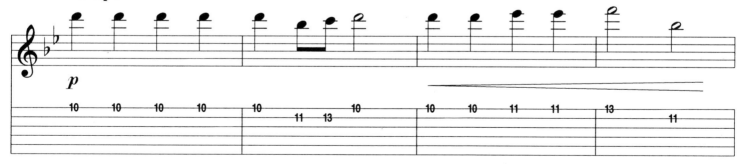

Song Of India

NIKOLAY ANDREYEVICH RIMSKY-KORSAKOV

Guitar
Andantino

*The tablature staff displays the most accessible fingering for the beginning student, which may vary from those chosen by the soloist.

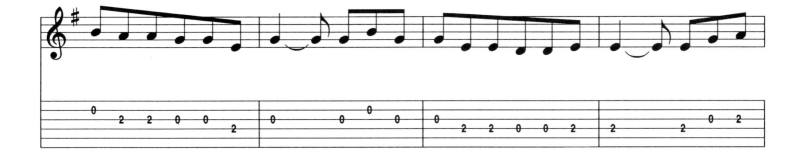

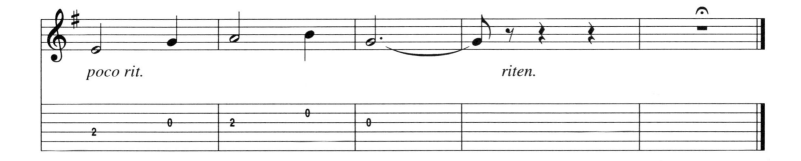

poco rit.   *riten.*

La Paloma

The Dove

SEBASTIAN IRADIER

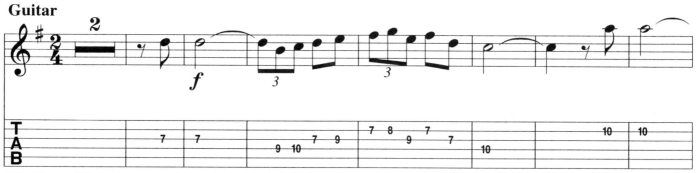

*The tablature staff displays the most accessible fingering for the beginning student, which may vary from those chosen by the soloist.

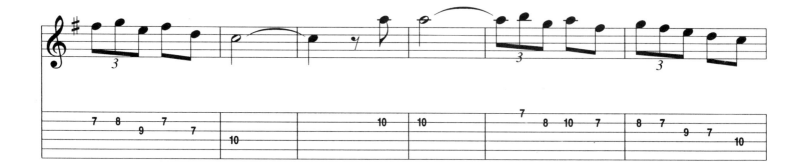

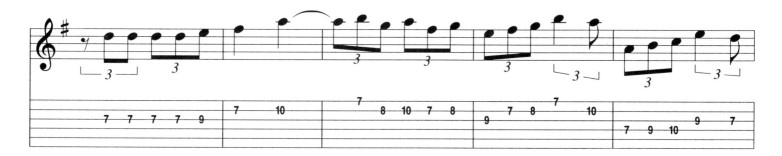

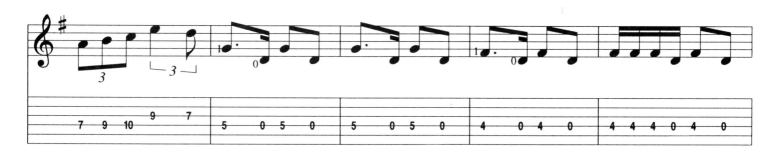

Vilia

The Merry Widow

FRANZ LEHAR

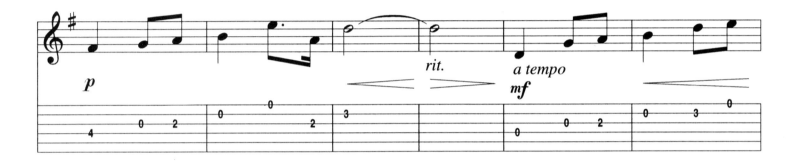

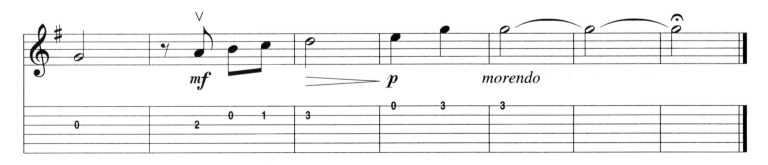

Adagietto
l'Arlesienne Suite

GEORGES BIZET

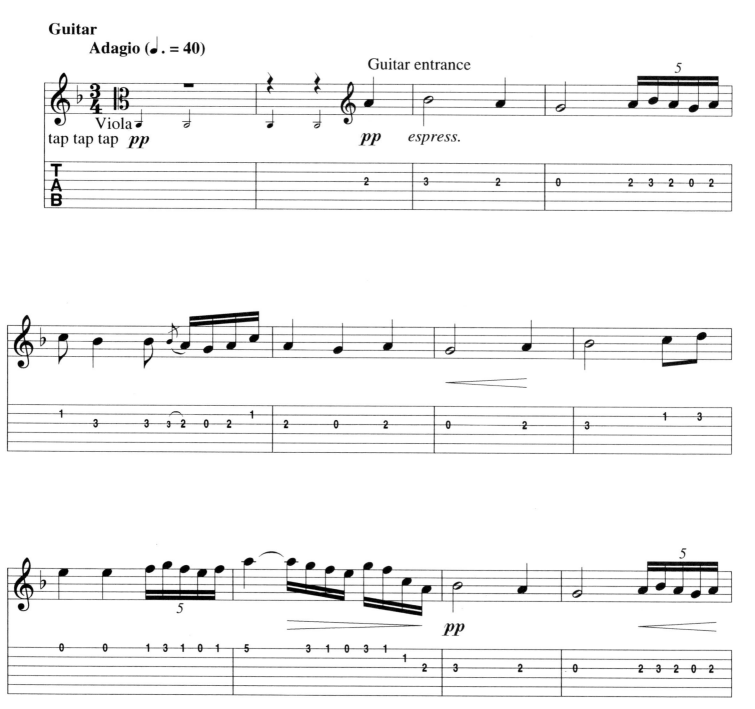

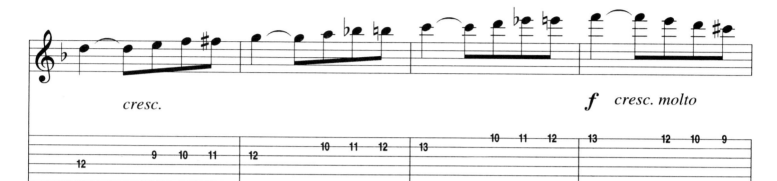

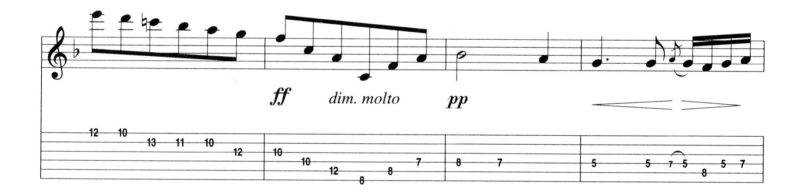

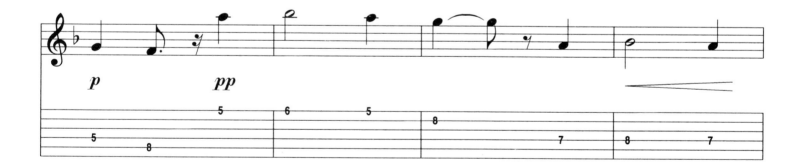

Old Folks At Home

STEPHEN FOSTER

*The tablature staff displays the most accessible fingering for the beginning student, which may vary from those chosen by the soloist.

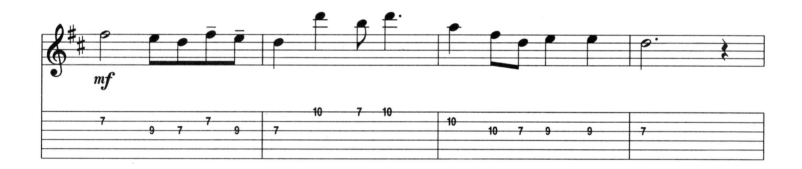

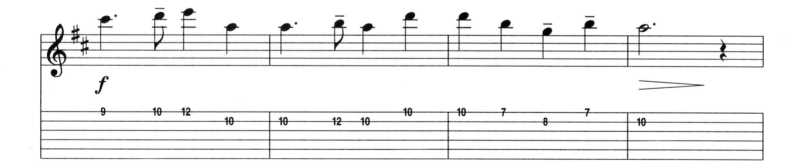

Drink To Me Only With Thine Eyes

TRADITIONAL

Moderato

Guitar

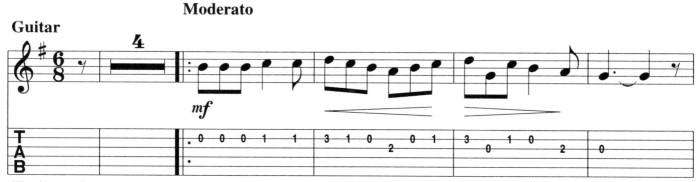

*The tablature staff displays the most accessible fingering for the beginning student, which may vary from those chosen by the soloist.

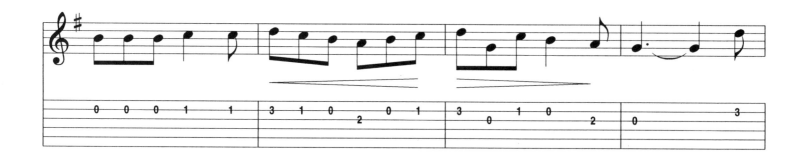

Silent Night

FRANZ GRUBER

Guitar
Moderato

*The tablature staff displays the most accessible fingering for the beginning student, which may vary from those chosen by the soloist.

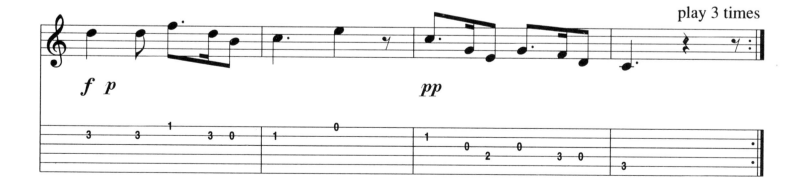

Barcarolle
Tales of Hoffman

JULES OFFENBACH

*The tablature staff displays the most accessible fingering for the beginning student, which may vary from those chosen by the soloist.

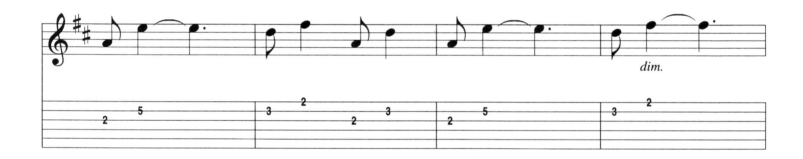

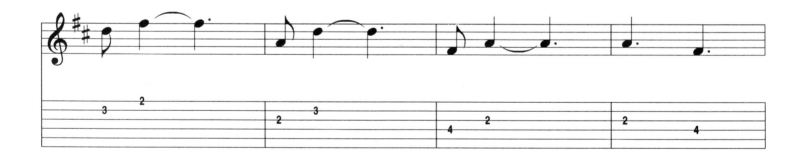

MMO Compact Disc Catalog

BROADWAY

LES MISERABLES/PHANTOM OF THE OPERA	MMO CD 1016
HITS OF ANDREW LLOYD WEBBER	MMO CD 1054
GUYS AND DOLLS	MMO CD 1067
WEST SIDE STORY 2 CD Set	MMO CD 1100
CABARET 2 CD Set	MMO CD 1110
BROADWAY HEROES AND HEROINES	MMO CD 1121
CAMELOT	MMO CD 1173
BEST OF ANDREW LLOYD WEBBER	MMO CD 1130
THE SOUND OF BROADWAY	MMO CD 1133
BROADWAY MELODIES	MMO CD 1134
BARBRA'S BROADWAY	MMO CD 1144
JEKYLL & HYDE	MMO CD 1151
SHOWBOAT	MMO CD 1160
MY FAIR LADY 2 CD Set	MMO CD 1174
OKLAHOMA!	MMO CD 1175
THE SOUND OF MUSIC 2 CD Set	MMO CD 1176
SOUTH PACIFIC	MMO CD 1177
THE KING AND I	MMO CD 1178
FIDDLER ON THE ROOF 2 CD Set	MMO CD 1179
CAROUSEL	MMO CD 1180
PORGY AND BESS	MMO CD 1181
THE MUSIC MAN	MMO CD 1183
ANNIE GET YOUR GUN 2 CD Set	MMO CD 1186
HELLO DOLLY! 2 CD Set	MMO CD 1187
OLIVER 2 CD Set	MMO CD 1189
SUNSET BOULEVARD	MMO CD 1193
GREASE	MMO CD 1196
SMOKEY JOE'S CAFE	MMO CD 1197

CLARINET

MOZART CONCERTO, IN A	MMO CD 3201
WEBER CONCERTO NO. 1 IN FM. STAMITZ CON. NO. 3 IN BB	MMO CD 3202
SPOHR CONCERTO NO. 1 IN C MINOR OP. 26	MMO CD 3203
WEBER CONCERTO OP. 26, BEETHOVEN TRIO OP. 11	MMO CD 3204
FIRST CHAIR CLARINET SOLOS	MMO CD 3205
THE ART OF THE SOLO CLARINET	MMO CD 3206
MOZART QUINTET IN A, K.581	MMO CD 3207
BRAHMS SONATAS OP. 120 NO. 1 & 2	MMO CD 3208
WEBER GRAND DUO CONCERTANT WAGNER ADAGIO	MMO CD 3209
SCHUMANN FANTASY OP. 73, 3 ROMANCES OP. 94	MMO CD 3210
EASY CLARINET SOLOS Volume 1 - STUDENT LEVEL	MMO CD 3211
EASY CLARINET SOLOS Volume 2 - STUDENT LEVEL	MMO CD 3212
EASY JAZZ DUETS - STUDENT LEVEL	MMO CD 3213
BEGINNING CONTEST SOLOS - Jerome Bunke, Clinician	MMO CD 3221
BEGINNING CONTEST SOLOS - Harold Wright	MMO CD 3222
INTERMEDIATE CONTEST SOLOS - Stanley Drucker	MMO CD 3223
INTERMEDIATE CONTEST SOLOS - Jerome Bunke, Clinician	MMO CD 3224
ADVANCED CONTEST SOLOS - Stanley Drucker	MMO CD 3225
ADVANCED CONTEST SOLOS - Harold Wright	MMO CD 3226
INTERMEDIATE CONTEST SOLOS - Stanley Drucker	MMO CD 3227
ADVANCED CONTEST SOLOS - Stanley Drucker	MMO CD 3228
ADVANCED CONTEST SOLOS - Harold Wright	MMO CD 3229
BRAHMS Clarinet Quintet in Am, Op. 115	MMO CD 3230
JEWELS FOR WOODWIND QUINTET	MMO CD 3232
WOODWIND QUINTETS minus CLARINET	MMO CD 3233

PIANO

BEETHOVEN CONCERTO NO 1 IN C	MMO CD 3001
BEETHOVEN CONCERTO NO. 2 IN Bb	MMO CD 3002
BEETHOVEN CONCERTO NO. 3 IN C MINOR	MMO CD 3003
BEETHOVEN CONCERTO NO. 4 IN G	MMO CD 3004
BEETHOVEN CONCERTO NO. 5 IN Eb (2 CD SET)	MMO CD 3005
GRIEG CONCERTO IN A MINOR OP.16	MMO CD 3006
RACHMANINOFF CONCERTO NO. 2 IN C MINOR	MMO CD 3007
SCHUMANN CONCERTO IN A MINOR	MMO CD 3008
BRAHMS CONCERTO NO. 1 IN D MINOR (2 CD SET)	MMO CD 3009
CHOPIN CONCERTO NO. 1 IN E MINOR OP. 11	MMO CD 3010
MENDELSSOHN CONCERTO NO. 1 IN G MINOR	MMO CD 3011
MOZART CONCERTO NO. 9 IN Eb K.271	MMO CD 3012
MOZART CONCERTO NO. 12 IN A K.414	MMO CD 3013
MOZART CONCERTO NO. 20 IN D MINOR K.466	MMO CD 3014
MOZART CONCERTO NO. 23 IN A K.488	MMO CD 3015
MOZART CONCERTO NO. 24 IN C MINOR K.491	MMO CD 3016
MOZART CONCERTO NO. 26 IN D K.537, CORONATION	MMO CD 3017
MOZART CONCERTO NO. 17 IN G K.453	MMO CD 3018
LISZT CONCERTO NO. 1 IN Eb, WEBER OP. 79	MMO CD 3019
LISZT CONCERTO NO. 2 IN A, HUNGARIAN FANTASIA	MMO CD 3020
J.S. BACH CONCERTO IN F MINOR, J.C. BACH CON. IN Eb	MMO CD 3021
J.S. BACH CONCERTO IN D MINOR	MMO CD 3022
HAYDN CONCERTO IN D	MMO CD 3023
HEART OF THE PIANO CONCERTO	MMO CD 3024
THEMES FROM GREAT PIANO CONCERTI	MMO CD 3025
TSCHAIKOVSKY CONCERTO NO. 1 IN Bb MINOR	MMO CD 3026
ART OF POPULAR PIANO PLAYING, Vol. 1 STUDENT LEVEL	MMO CD 3033
ART OF POPULAR PIANO PLAYING, Vol. 2 STUDENT LEVEL 2 CD Set	MMO CD 3034
'POP' PIANO FOR STARTERS STUDENT LEVEL	MMO CD 3035
MOZART COMPLETE MUSIC FOR PIANO FOUR HANDS 2 CD Set	MMO CD 3036

INSTRUCTIONAL METHODS

RUTGERS UNIVERSITY MUSIC DICTATION/EAR TRAINING COURSE (7 CD Set)	MMO CD 7001
EVOLUTION OF THE BLUES	MMO CD 7004
THE ART OF IMPROVISATION, VOL. 1	MMO CD 7005
THE ART OF IMPROVISATION, VOL. 2	MMO CD 7006
THE BLUES MINUS YOU Ed Xiques, Soloist	MMO CD 7007
TAKE A CHORUS minus Bb/Eb Instruments	MMO CD 7008

VIOLIN

BRUCH CONCERTO NO. 1 IN G MINOR OP.26	MMO CD 3100
MENDELSSOHN CONCERTO IN E MINOR	MMO CD 3101
TSCHAIKOVSKY CONCERTO IN D OP. 35	MMO CD 3102
BACH DOUBLE CONCERTO IN D MINOR	MMO CD 3103
BACH CONCERTO IN A MINOR, CONCERTO IN E	MMO CD 3104
BACH BRANDENBURG CONCERTI NOS. 4 & 5	MMO CD 3105
BACH BRANDENBURG CONCERTO NO. 2, TRIPLE CONCERTO	MMO CD 3106
BACH CONCERTO IN DM, (FROM CONCERTO FOR HARPSICHORD)	MMO CD 3107
BRAHMS CONCERTO IN D OP. 77	MMO CD 3108
CHAUSSON POEME, SCHUBERT RONDO	MMO CD 3109
LALO SYMPHONIE ESPAGNOLE	MMO CD 3110
MOZART CONCERTO IN D K.218, VIVALDI CON. AM OP.3 NO.6	MMO CD 3111
MOZART CONCERTO IN A K.219	MMO CD 3112
WIENIAWSKI CON. IN D. SARASATE ZIGEUNERWEISEN	MMO CD 3113
VIOTTI CONCERTO NO.22	MMO CD 3114
BEETHOVEN 2 ROMANCES, SONATA NO. 5 IN F "SPRING SONATA"	MMO CD 3115
SAINT-SAENS INTRODUCTION & RONDO, MOZART SERENADE K. 204, ADAGIO K.261	MMO CD 3116
BEETHOVEN CONCERTO IN D OP. 61(2 CD SET)	MMO CD 3117
THE CONCERTMASTER	MMO CD 3118
AIR ON A G STRING Favorite Encores with Orchestra Easy Medium	MMO CD 3119
CONCERT PIECES FOR THE SERIOUS VIOLINIST Easy Medium	MMO CD 3120
18TH CENTURY VIOLIN PIECES	MMO CD 3121
ORCHESTRAL FAVORITES - Volume 1 - Easy Level	MMO CD 3122
ORCHESTRAL FAVORITES - Volume 2 - Medium Level	MMO CD 3123
ORCHESTRAL FAVORITES - Volume 3 - Med to Difficult Level	MMO CD 3124
THE THREE B'S BACH/BEETHOVEN/BRAHMS	MMO CD 3125
VIVALDI Concerto in A Minor Op. 3 No. 6. in D Op. 3 No. 9. Double Concerto Op. 3 No. 8	MMO CD 3126
VIVALDI-THE FOUR SEASONS (2 CD Set)	MMO CD 3127
VIVALDI Concerto in Eb, Op. 8, No. 5. ALBINONI Concerto in A	MMO CD 3128
VIVALDI Concerto in E, Op. 3, No. 12. Concerto in C Op. 8, No. 6 "Il Piacere"	MMO CD 3129
SCHUBERT Three Sonatinas	MMO CD 3130
HAYDN String Quartet Op. 76 No. 1	MMO CD 3131
HAYDN String Quartet Op. 76 No. 2	MMO CD 3132
HAYDN String Quartet Op. 76 No. 3 "Emperor"	MMO CD 3133
HAYDN String Quartet Op. 76 No. 4 "Sunrise"	MMO CD 3134
HAYDN String Quartet Op. 76 No. 5	MMO CD 3135
HAYDN String Quartet Op. 76 No. 6	MMO CD 3136
BEAUTIFUL MUSIC FOR TWO VIOLINS 1st position, vol. 1	MMO CD 3137
BEAUTIFUL MUSIC FOR TWO VIOLINS 2nd position, vol. 2	MMO CD 3138
BEAUTIFUL MUSIC FOR TWO VIOLINS 3rd position, vol. 3	MMO CD 3139
BEAUTIFUL MUSIC FOR TWO VIOLINS 1st, 2nd, 3rd position, vol. 4	MMO CD 3140
DVORAK Terzetto	MMO CD 3142

Lovely folk tunes and selections from the classics, chosen for their melodic beauty and technical value. They have been skillfully transcribed and edited by Samuel Applebaum, one of America's foremost teachers.

CELLO

DVORAK Concerto in B Minor Op. 104 (2 CD Set)	MMO CD 3701
C.P.E. BACH Concerto in A Minor	MMO CD 3702
BOCCHERINI Concerto in Bb, BRUCH Kol Nidrei	MMO CD 3703
TEN PIECES FOR CELLO	MMO CD 3704
SCHUMANN Concerto in Am & Other Selections	MMO CD 3705
CLAUDE BOLLING Suite For Cello & Jazz Piano Trio	MMO CD 3706

OBOE

ALBINONI Concerti in Bb, Op. 7 No. 3, No. 6, Dm Op. 9 No. 2.	MMO CD 3400
TELEMANN Conc. in Fm; HANDEL Conc. in Bb; VIVALDI Conc.in Dm	MMO CD 3401
MOZART Quartet in F K.370, STAMITZ Quartet in F Op. 8 No. 3	MMO CD 3402
BACH Brandenburg Concerto No. 2, Telemann Con. in Am	MMO CD 3403
CLASSIC SOLOS FOR OBOE Delia Montenegro, Soloist	MMO CD 3404
MASTERPIECES FOR WOODWIND QUINTET	MMO CD 3405
WOODWIND QUINTETS minus OBOE	MMO CD 3406

GUITAR

BOCCHERINI Quintet No. 4 in D "Fandango"	MMO CD 3601
GIULIANI Quintet in A Op. 65	MMO CD 3602
CLASSICAL GUITAR DUETS	MMO CD 3603
RENAISSANCE & BAROQUE GUITAR DUETS	MMO CD 3604
CLASSICAL & ROMANTIC GUITAR DUETS	MMO CD 3605
GUITAR AND FLUTE DUETS Volume 1	MMO CD 3606
GUITAR AND FLUTE DUETS Volume 2	MMO CD 3607
BLUEGRASS GUITAR CLASSIC PIECES minus you	MMO CD 3608
GEORGE BARNES GUITAR METHOD Lessons from a Master	MMO CD 3609
HOW TO PLAY FOLK GUITAR 2 CD Set	MMO CD 3610
FAVORITE FOLKS SONGS FOR GUITAR	MMO CD 3611
FOR GUITARS ONLY! Jimmy Raney Small Band Arrangements	MMO CD 3612
TEN DUETS FOR TWO GUITARS Geo. Barnes/Carl Kress	MMO CD 3613
PLAY THE BLUES GUITAR A Dick Weissman Method	MMO CD 3614
ORCHESTRAL GEMS FOR CLASSICAL GUITAR	MMO CD 3615

BANJO

BLUEGRASS BANJO Classic & Favorite Banjo Pieces	MMO CD 4401
PLAY THE FIVE STRING BANJO Vol. 1 Dick Weissman Method	MMO CD 4402
PLAY THE FIVE STRING BANJO Vol. 2 Dick Weissman Method	MMO CD 4403

MMO CD 3615

FLUTE

MOZART Concerto No. 2 in D, QUANTZ Concerto in G ....MMO CD 3300
MOZART Concerto in G K.313 ....MMO CD 3301
BACH Suite No. 2 in B Minor ....MMO CD 3302
BOCCHERINI Concerto in D, VIVALDI Concerto in G Minor "La Notte",
MOZART Andante for Strings ....MMO CD 3303
HAYDN Divertimento, VIVALDI Concerto in D Op. 10 No. 3 "Bullfinch",
FREDERICK THE GREAT Concerto in C ....MMO CD 3304
VIVALDI Conc. in F; TELEMANN Conc. in D; LECLAIR Conc. in C ....MMO CD 3305
BACH Brandenburg No. 2 in F, HAYDN Concerto in D ....MMO CD 3306
BACH Triple Concerto, VIVALDI Concerto in D Minor ....MMO CD 3307
MOZART Quartet in F, STAMITZ Quartet in F ....MMO CD 3308
HAYDN 4 London Trios for 2 Flutes & Cello ....MMO CD 3309
BACH Brandenburg Concerti Nos. 4 & 5 ....MMO CD 3310
MOZART 3 Flute Quartets in D, A and C ....MMO CD 3311
TELEMANN Suite in A Minor, GLUCK Scene from 'Orpheus',
PERGOLESI Concerto in G   2 CD Set ....MMO CD 3312
FLUTE SONG: Easy Familiar Classics ....MMO CD 3313
VIVALDI Concerti in D, G, and F ....MMO CD 3314
VIVALDI Concerti in A Minor, G, and D ....MMO CD 3315
EASY FLUTE SOLOS Beginning Students Volume 1 ....MMO CD 3316
EASY FLUTE SOLOS Beginning Students Volume 2 ....MMO CD 3317
EASY JAZZ DUETS Student Level ....MMO CD 3318
FLUTE & GUITAR DUETS Volume 1 ....MMO CD 3319
FLUTE & GUITAR DUETS Volume 2 ....MMO CD 3320
BEGINNING CONTEST SOLOS Murray Panitz ....MMO CD 3321
BEGINNING CONTEST SOLOS Donald Peck ....MMO CD 3322
INTERMEDIATE CONTEST SOLOS Julius Baker ....MMO CD 3323
INTERMEDIATE CONTEST SOLOS Donald Peck ....MMO CD 3324
ADVANCED CONTEST SOLOS Murray Panitz ....MMO CD 3325
ADVANCED CONTEST SOLOS Julius Baker ....MMO CD 3326
INTERMEDIATE CONTEST SOLOS Donald Peck ....MMO CD 3327
ADVANCED CONTEST SOLOS Murray Panitz ....MMO CD 3328
INTERMEDIATE CONTEST SOLOS Julius Baker ....MMO CD 3329
BEGINNING CONTEST SOLOS Doriot Anthony Dwyer ....MMO CD 3330
INTERMEDIATE CONTEST SOLOS Doriot Anthony Dwyer ....MMO CD 3331
ADVANCED CONTEST SOLOS Doriot Anthony Dwyer ....MMO CD 3332
FIRST CHAIR SOLOS with Orchestral Accompaniment ....MMO CD 3333
THE JOY OF WOODWIND MUSIC ....MMO CD 3335
WOODWIND QUINTETS minus FLUTE ....MMO CD 3336

RECORDER

PLAYING THE RECORDER Folk Songs of Many Naitons ....MMO CD 3337
LET'S PLAY THE RECORDER Beginning Children's Method ....MMO CD 3338
YOU CAN PLAY THE RECORDER Beginning Adult Method ....MMO CD 3339

FRENCH HORN

MOZART Concerti No. 2 & No. 3 in Eb. K. 417 & 447 ....MMO CD 3501
BAROQUE BRASS AND BEYOND ....MMO CD 3502
MUSIC FOR BRASS ENSEMBLE ....MMO CD 3503
MOZART Sonatas for Two Horns ....MMO CD 3504
BEGINNING CONTEST SOLOS Mason Jones ....MMO CD 3511
BEGINNING CONTEST SOLOS Myron Bloom ....MMO CD 3512
INTERMEDIATE CONTEST SOLOS Dale Clevenger ....MMO CD 3513
INTERMEDIATE CONTEST SOLOS Mason Jones ....MMO CD 3514
ADVANCED CONTEST SOLOS Myron Bloom ....MMO CD 3515
ADVANCED CONTEST SOLOS Dale Clevenger ....MMO CD 3516
INTERMEDIATE CONTEST SOLOS Mason Jones ....MMO CD 3517
ADVANCED CONTEST SOLOS Myron Bloom ....MMO CD 3518
INTERMEDIATE CONTEST SOLOS Dale Clevenger ....MMO CD 3519
FRENCH HORN WOODWIND MUSIC ....MMO CD 3520
WOODWIND QUINTETS minus FRENCH HORN ....MMO CD 3521

TRUMPET

THREE CONCERTI: HAYDN, TELEMANN, FASCH ....MMO CD 3801
TRUMPET SOLOS Student Level Volume 1 ....MMO CD 3802
TRUMPET SOLOS Student Level Volume 2 ....MMO CD 3803
EASY JAZZ DUETS Student Level ....MMO CD 3804
MUSIC FOR BRASS ENSEMBLE Brass Quintets ....MMO CD 3805
FIRST CHAIR TRUMPET SOLOS with Orchestral Accompaniment ....MMO CD 3806
THE ART OF THE SOLO TRUMPET with Orchestral Accompaniment ....MMO CD 3807
BAROQUE BRASS AND BEYOND Brass Quintets ....MMO CD 3808
THE COMPLETE ARBAN DUETS all of the classic studies ....MMO CD 3809
SOUSA MARCHES PLUS BEETHOVEN, BERLIOZ, STRAUSS ....MMO CD 3810
BEGINNING CONTEST SOLOS Gerard Schwarz ....MMO CD 3811
BEGINNING CONTEST SOLOS Armando Ghitalla ....MMO CD 3812
INTERMEDIATE CONTEST SOLOS Robert Nagel, Soloist ....MMO CD 3813
INTERMEDIATE CONTEST SOLOS Gerard Schwarz ....MMO CD 3814
ADVANCED CONTEST SOLOS Robert Nagel, Soloist ....MMO CD 3815
ADVANCED CONTEST SOLOS Armando Ghitalla ....MMO CD 3816
INTERMEDIATE CONTEST SOLOS Gerard Schwarz ....MMO CD 3817
ADVANCED CONTEST SOLOS Robert Nagel, Soloist ....MMO CD 3818
ADVANCED CONTEST SOLOS Armando Ghilalla ....MMO CD 3819
BEGINNING CONTEST SOLOS Raymond Crisara ....MMO CD 3820
BEGINNING CONTEST SOLOS Raymond Crisara ....MMO CD 3821
INTERMEDIATE CONTEST SOLOS Raymond Crisara ....MMO CD 3822

TROMBONE

TROMBONE SOLOS Student Level Volume 1 ....MMO CD 3901
TROMBONE SOLOS Student Level Volume 2 ....MMO CD 3902
EASY JAZZ DUETS Student Level ....MMO CD 3903
BAROQUE BRASS & BEYOND Brass Quintets ....MMO CD 3904
MUSIC FOR BRASS ENSEMBLE Brass Quintets ....MMO CD 3905
BEGINNING CONTEST SOLOS Per Brevig ....MMO CD 3911
BEGINNING CONTEST SOLOS Jay Friedman ....MMO CD 3912
INTERMEDIATE CONTEST SOLOS Keith Brown, Professor, Indiana University ....MMO CD 3913
INTERMEDIATE CONTEST SOLOS Jay Friedman ....MMO CD 3914

ADVANCED CONTEST SOLOS Keith Brown, Professor, Indiana University ....MMO CD 3915
ADVANCED CONTEST SOLOS Per Brevig ....MMO CD 3916
ADVANCED CONTEST SOLOS Keith Brown, Professor, Indiana University ....MMO CD 3917
ADVANCED CONTEST SOLOS Jay Friedman ....MMO CD 3918
ADVANCED CONTEST SOLOS Per Brevig ....MMO CD 3919

DOUBLE BASS

BEGINNING TO INTERMEDIATE CONTEST SOLOS David Walter ....MMO CD 4301
INTERMEDIATE TO ADVANCED CONTEST SOLOS David Walter ....MMO CD 4302
FOR BASSISTS ONLY Ken Smith, Soloist ....MMO CD 4303
THE BEAT GOES ON Jazz - Funk, Latin, Pop-Rock ....MMO CD 4304

TENOR SAX

TENOR SAXOPHONE SOLOS Student Edition Volume 1 ....MMO CD 4201
TENOR SAXOPHONE SOLOS Student Edition Volume 2 ....MMO CD 4202
EASY JAZZ DUETS FOR TENOR SAXOPHONE ....MMO CD 4203
FOR SAXES ONLY Arranged by Bob Wilber ....MMO CD 4204

ALTO SAXOPHONE

ALTO SAXOPHONE SOLOS Student Edition Volume 1 ....MMO CD 4101
ALTO SAXOPHONE SOLOS Student Edition Volume 2 ....MMO CD 4102
EASY JAZZ DUETS FOR ALTO SAXOPHONE ....MMO CD 4103
FOR SAXES ONLY Arranged Bob Wilber ....MMO CD 4104
BEGINNING CONTEST SOLOS Paul Brodie, Canadian Soloist ....MMO CD 4111
BEGINNING CONTEST SOLOS Vincent Abato ....MMO CD 4112
INTERMEDIATE CONTEST SOLOS Paul Brodie, Canadian Soloist ....MMO CD 4113
INTERMEDIATE CONTEST SOLOS Vincent Abato ....MMO CD 4114
ADVANCED CONTEST SOLOS Paul Brodie. Canadian Soloist ....MMO CD 4115
ADVANCED CONTEST SOLOS Vincent Abato ....MMO CD 4116
ADVANCED CONTEST SOLOS Paul Brodie, Canadian Soloist ....MMO CD 4117
ADVANCED CONTEST SOLOS Vincent Abato ....MMO CD 4118

DRUMS

MODERN JAZZ DRUMMING 2 CD Set ....MMO CD 5001
FOR DRUMMERS ONLY ....MMO CD 5002
WIPE OUT ....MMO CD 5003
SIT-IN WITH JIM CHAPIN ....MMO CD 5004
DRUM STAR Trios/Quartets/Quintets Minus You ....MMO CD 5005
DRUMPADSTICKSKIN Jazz play-alongs with small groups ....MMO CD 5006
CLASSICAL PERCUSSION 2 CD Set ....MMO CD 5009
EIGHT MEN IN SEARCH OF A DRUMMER ....MMO CD 5010

VOCAL

SCHUBERT GERMAN LIEDER - High Voice, Volume 1 ....MMO CD 4001
SCHUBERT GERMAN LIEDER - Low Voice, Volume 1 ....MMO CD 4002
SCHUBERT GERMAN LIEDER - High Voice, Volume 2 ....MMO CD 4003
SCHUBERT GERMAN LIEDER - Low Voice, Volume 2 ....MMO CD 4004
BRAHMS GERMAN LIEDER - High Voice ....MMO CD 4005
BRAHMS GERMAN LIEDER - Low Voice ....MMO CD 4006
EVERYBODY'S FAVORITE SONGS - High Voice, Volume 1 ....MMO CD 4007
EVERYBODY'S FAVORITE SONGS - Low Voice, Volume 1 ....MMO CD 4008
EVERYBODY'S FAVORITE SONGS - High Voice, Volume 2 ....MMO CD 4009
EVERYBODY'S FAVORITE SONGS - Low Voice, Volume 2 ....MMO CD 4010
17th/18th CENT. ITALIAN SONGS - High Voice, Volume 1 ....MMO CD 4011
17th/18th CENT. ITALIAN SONGS - Low Voice, Volume 1 ....MMO CD 4012
17th/18th CENT. ITALIAN SONGS - High Voice, Volume 2 ....MMO CD 4013
17th/18th CENT. ITALIAN SONGS - Low Voice, Volume 2 ....MMO CD 4014
FAMOUS SOPRANO ARIAS ....MMO CD 4015
FAMOUS MEZZO-SOPRANO ARIAS ....MMO CD 4016
FAMOUS TENOR ARIAS ....MMO CD 4017
FAMOUS BARITONE ARIAS ....MMO CD 4018
FAMOUS BASS ARIAS ....MMO CD 4019
WOLF GERMAN LIEDER FOR HIGH VOICE ....MMO CD 4020
WOLF GERMAN LIEDER FOR LOW VOICE ....MMO CD 4021
STRAUSS GERMAN LIEDER FOR HIGH VOICE ....MMO CD 4022
STRAUSS GERMAN LIEDER FOR LOW VOICE ....MMO CD 4023
SCHUMANN GERMAN LIEDER FOR HIGH VOICE ....MMO CD 4024
SCHUMANN GERMAN LIEDER FOR LOW VOICE ....MMO CD 4025
MOZART ARIAS FOR SOPRANO ....MMO CD 4026
VERDI ARIAS FOR SOPRANO ....MMO CD 4027
ITALIAN ARIAS FOR SOPRANO ....MMO CD 4028
FRENCH ARIAS FOR SOPRANO ....MMO CD 4029
ORATORIO ARIAS FOR SOPRANO ....MMO CD 4030
ORATORIO ARIAS FOR ALTO ....MMO CD 4031
ORATORIO ARIAS FOR TENOR ....MMO CD 4032
ORATORIO ARIAS FOR BASS ....MMO CD 4033
BEGINNING SOPRANO SOLOS Kate Hurney ....MMO CD 4041
INTERMEDIATE SOPRANO SOLOS Kate Hurney ....MMO CD 4042
BEGINNING MEZZO SOPRANO SOLOS Fay Kittelson ....MMO CD 4043
INTERMEDIATE MEZZO SOPRANO SOLOS Fay Kittelson ....MMO CD 4044
ADVANCED MEZZO SOPRANO SOLOS Fay Kittelson ....MMO CD 4045
BEGINNING CONTRALTO SOLOS Carline Ray ....MMO CD 4046
BEGINNING TENOR SOLOS George Shirley ....MMO CD 4047
INTERMEDIATE TENOR SOLOS George Shirley ....MMO CD 4048
ADVANCED TENOR SOLOS George Shirley ....MMO CD 4049

BASSOON

SOLOS FOR THE BASSOON Janet Grice, Soloist ....MMO CD 4601
MASTERPIECES FOR WOODWIND MUSIC ....MMO CD 4602
WOODWIND QUINTETS minus BASSOON ....MMO CD 4603

VIOLA

VIOLA SOLOS with piano accompaniment ....MMO CD 4501
DVORAK QUINTET IN A, Opus 81 ....MMO CD 4502
DVORAK TRIO "Terzetto" 2 Vins/Viola ....MMO CD 4503

MMO MUSIC GROUP, INC., 50 Executive Boulevard, Elmsford, NY 10523-1325